Amish Soups
& Casseroles

Amish Soups & Casseroles

TRADITIONAL COMFORT FOOD FAVORITES

Linda Byler, Laura Anne Lapp, Emily Stoltzfus & Anna Kauffman

Photos by Bonnie Matthews

Good Books
New York, New York

Good Books books may be purchased in bulk at special discounts for sales promotion, corporate gifts, fund-raising, or educational purposes. Special editions can also be created to specifications. For details, contact the Special Sales Department, Good Books, 307 West 36th Street, 11th Floor, New York, NY 10018 or info@skyhorsepublishing.com.

Good Books is an imprint of Skyhorse Publishing, Inc.®, a Delaware corporation.

Visit our website at www.goodbooks.com.

10 9 8 7 6 5 4 3

Library of Congress Cataloging-in-Publication Data is available on file.

ISBN: 978-1-68099-841-2
eBook ISBN: 978-1-68099-850-4

Cover design by David Ter-Avanesyan
Cover photograph by Bonnie Matthews

Printed in China

"I still think of food, love, and my mother as exactly the same thing."
—Linda Byler

CONTENTS

INTRODUCTION

The recipes in this cookbook bring warmth to my heart as I remember our suppers in the old farmhouse on Weaver Road. My mother (Anna Kauffman) was a wonderful cook, making do with the modest grocery funds available, turning a bit of ground beef, potatoes, and green beans into a solid, rib-sticking meal. There were ten children around the dining room table, with my father at the far end. Mam sat on his right side and the rest of us were seated on benches along the side. I remember suppers with mounds of mashed potatoes, ground beef gravy, green beans in a white sauce, and homemade bread with margarine and strawberry jelly (real butter was only for special occasions). We were happy as larks. Other favorites included beef stew and homemade dumplings with applesauce, home-canned pickles and relishes, red beet eggs, fried chicken, and brown butter noodles—all of it comforting, filling, and home-cooked. Those suppers in the old dining room on the farm are some of my happiest memories.

Many of the recipes in this book come from my mother's tin box, the recipe cards dog-eared and faded. I can still see her kneading bread dough, her gray apron tied around her soft waist, the color in her face heightened on account of the woodstove beside her. We were poor, but rich in all the things that make life happy.

Other recipes in this book come from my daughters, Laura and Emily, who are excellent cooks and now provide wonderful meals for their own families. It's a joy to see them carrying on the traditions of home-cooked meals and family suppers. Perhaps our recipes will inspire you to share a warm meal with *your* loved ones and create your own lasting memories.

—Linda Byler

Soups & Stews

CHICKEN CORN SOUP

Makes 6 servings

Ingredients:

4 tablespoons butter

¾–1 cup chopped celery

¾–1 cup chopped onion

3–4 cups water

1 quart corn

4 cups cooked and diced chicken

6–7 teaspoons chicken bouillon

2 tablespoons parsley flakes

1 tablespoon salt

½–1 teaspoon pepper

4 ounces uncooked noodles, *optional*

Instructions:

1. Melt butter in large saucepan.

2. Cook celery and onion in butter until soft.

3. Add water.

4. Stir in corn, chicken, chicken bouillon, parsley, salt, and pepper. Bring to a boil.

5. Add noodles if you wish. Allow to simmer until noodles are tender, about 10 more minutes.

Tip: Add more water and chicken bouillon if necessary to have the consistency and flavor of soup that you like.

HAM, GREEN BEANS, AND POTATO STEW

Makes 8 servings

Ingredients:
4 cups cooked and cubed ham
4 cups cubed raw potatoes
2 quarts ham broth, *or* water
1 quart canned, *or* fresh, green beans
Salt and pepper to taste

Instructions:

1. Cook ham, potatoes, and broth in large stockpot until potatoes are soft.

2. Add green beans. Heat through if using canned beans. If using fresh beans, cook until beans are as tender as you like them.

3. Sprinkle with salt and pepper.

4. Stir to combine.

HAM CHOWDER

Makes 4–6 servings

Ingredients:

4 tablespoons butter
½ cup minced onions
½ cup chopped celery
1 cup cooked and diced ham
2 cups peeled and diced potatoes
½ cup water
3 tablespoons flour
1½ teaspoons salt
¼ teaspoon pepper
5 cups milk

Instructions:

1. Melt butter in large saucepan.

2. Add onions, celery, and ham.

3. Cook until onions and celery are soft.

4. Add potatoes and ½ cup water.

5. Cook 10 minutes, or until potatoes are soft.

6. Stir in flour, salt, and pepper until well blended.

7. Stir in milk until well blended.

8. Let simmer 15 minutes. Stir frequently to make sure the chowder's creamy base is smooth and thickened.

HAM AND CHEESE CHOWDER

Makes 8–10 servings

Ingredients:

3 quarts water
4 potatoes, diced
1 cup chopped carrots
1 cup chopped celery
2 teaspoons salt
¼ teaspoon pepper
½ cup (1 stick) butter
½ cup all-purpose flour
1 quart milk
1 pound Velveeta or American cheese
2 pounds fully cooked and cubed ham

Instructions:

1. Bring 3 quarts water to a boil. Add potatoes, carrots, celery, salt, and pepper. Boil until potatoes are tender. Drain.

2. In a large pot or Dutch oven, melt butter and mix in the flour. Gradually stir in the milk.

3. Add drained veggies and bring to a boil, stirring constantly.

4. Add cheese and stir until melted.

5. Add ham and simmer until heated through.

HAM AND BEAN SOUP

Makes 8–10 servings

Ingredients:

8 cups fully cooked and cubed ham

4 cups diced onions

½ cup (1 stick) butter

2 quarts water

4 quarts cooked Northern beans, drained

Instructions:

1. In a 12-quart stockpot, cook ham and onions in butter until onions are soft.

2. Add water and beans.

3. Cover. Over medium heat, bring to a boil. Allow to simmer 30 minutes.

4. Stir from time to time. If soup thickens beyond what you like, add more water, 1–2 cups at a time.

CHEESEBURGER SOUP

Makes 8 servings

Ingredients:
½ pound ground beef
¾ cup chopped onions
¾ cup shredded carrots
¾ cup chopped celery
4 tablespoons butter, cut into pieces
1 teaspoon parsley
3 cups chicken broth
3 cups peeled and diced potatoes
¼ cup flour
2 cups cubed Velveeta cheese
1¾ cups milk
½ teaspoon salt
¼ teaspoon pepper
½ teaspoon celery salt

Instructions:

1. In large saucepan, brown ground beef. Stir frequently to break up clumps.

2. Add onions, carrots, celery, butter, and parsley. Cook until vegetables are soft.

3. In a separate bowl, combine remaining ingredients.

4. Pour over beef mixture.

5. Heat until boiling.

6. Reduce heat and simmer, covered, about 30–40 minutes, or until potatoes are soft.

BEEF VEGETABLE SOUP

Makes 12 servings

Ingredients:

2 pounds cubed stewing meat, cut into
  bite-sized pieces
1 quart tomato juice
⅓ cup chopped onion
1 teaspoon salt
¼ teaspoon chili powder
1 cup chopped celery
1 cup chopped raw carrots
2 cups diced raw potatoes
16-ounce can, *or* frozen package, corn
16-ounce can, *or* frozen package, green beans
8 cups water
16-ounce can, *or* frozen package, peas

Instructions:

1. In large saucepan, combine meat, tomato juice, onion, salt, and chili powder.

2. Cover and cook over medium-low heat for 1–2 hours, or just until meat is tender.

3. Skim off any fat that has surfaced.

4. Stir in all vegetables, except peas. Add water.

5. Cover and simmer 45–60 minutes, or until vegetables are soft.

6. Stir in peas and cook another 10–15 minutes, or until the peas are heated through.

Tips:
1. When making vegetable soup, use whatever vegetables you prefer or have on hand.
2. You can also use fresh, instead of canned or frozen, vegetables.

HAMBURGER VEGGIE SOUP

Makes 15–20 servings

Ingredients:

2½ quarts tomato juice

2 quarts cooked beans of your choice, drained,
  or 4 (15½-ounce) cans of beans of your choice,
  drained

2 cups chopped celery

2 cups sliced carrots

1 quart corn, or 2 (1-pound) packages frozen corn

4 cups peeled and cubed raw potatoes

1½ pounds ground beef

2 large bell peppers, chopped

2 large onions, chopped

2 tablespoons minced parsley

Instructions:

1. In large stockpot, mix together tomato juice, beans, celery, carrots, corn, and potatoes.

2. In skillet, cook ground beef, peppers, and onions together. Stir frequently to break up clumps of meat.

3. Drain ground beef and stir into soup.

4. Bring to a boil, then reduce heat and simmer until vegetables are as soft as you like them.

5. Top each bowl of soup with minced parsley.

CREAM OF TUNA SOUP

Makes 6 servings

Ingredients:

6-ounce can tuna, in water *or* oil
4 tablespoons butter
4 tablespoons flour
1 teaspoon salt
½ teaspoon pepper
6 cups milk, *divided*
¾ cup shredded cheese of your choice, *optional*

Instructions:

1. If using tuna in water, melt butter in saucepan. Drain tuna and fry lightly in butter. If using tuna in oil, simply fry tuna in the oil. No need to use butter.

2. Stir in flour, salt, and pepper. Blend well.

3. Over medium heat, add 2 cups of milk, stirring constantly. Cook until thickened.

4. Stir in remaining milk until well blended.

5. Heat, continuing to stir frequently, until hot but not boiling.

6. If you wish, stir shredded cheese into soup just before serving.

Cream of tuna soup was a good way to stretch a few can of inexpensive tuna, and it was a soup we all loved. With noodles and cheese, the soup would fill the copper-bottomed pot, Mam's soup kettle. We often ate it with saltines and applesauce. Mm-mm. —Linda

CREAM OF BROCCOLI SOUP

Makes 16 servings

Ingredients:

½ cup finely chopped onion
1 tablespoon butter
2 quarts chopped broccoli
1 tablespoon chicken bouillon
1 tablespoon salt
1 teaspoon pepper
1 gallon milk
1 tablespoon cheddar cheese powder
1 pound white American cheese
½ cup all-purpose flour
½ cup cornstarch

Instructions:

1. In a Dutch oven or stockpot, sauté onion in butter until fragrant and translucent.

2. Add broccoli and enough water to almost cover.

3. Add bouillon, salt, and pepper. Cook until broccoli is tender.

4. Add milk, cheese powder, and cheese. Heat to almost boiling.

5. Add flour. Mix cornstarch with enough water to form a paste, then add to soup. Heat and stir until soup thickens.

CHUNKY TOMATO SOUP

Makes 6–8 servings

Ingredients:

¼ cup chopped onions

2 tablespoons butter

1 quart home-canned, *or* 2 (15½-ounce) cans,
   stewed tomatoes, undrained

1 teaspoon salt

Pepper to taste

¼ teaspoon baking soda

2 quarts milk

Instructions:

1. In large stockpot, fry onions in butter until soft.

2. Add tomatoes, salt, pepper, and baking soda. Mix well.

3. Heat until boiling.

4. In separate saucepan, heat milk until almost boiling. Skin will form on top.

5. Remove from heat.

6. Pour hot milk into tomato mixture, stirring constantly.

7. Serve.

CREAMY TOMATO SOUP

Makes 4 servings

Ingredients:
4 tablespoons butter
4 tablespoons flour
½ teaspoon salt
4 cups milk
2 cups tomato juice

Instructions:

1. Melt butter in medium saucepan.

2. Stir in flour and salt until mixture is smooth.

3. Over medium heat, and stirring constantly, slowly pour in milk.

4. Cook, stirring continually, until thickened.

5. Slowly stir in tomato juice and heat until warm. Do not boil.

CREAMY TOMATO WITH RICE SOUP

Makes 8–10 servings

Ingredients:
½ cup diced onions
3 tablespoons butter
3 quarts diced tomatoes
1 quart tomato juice
1 cup water
1 tablespoon chicken bouillon
¼–½ cup sugar
1 teaspoon baking soda
1 quart half-and-half
2 cups heavy cream
2 cups milk
2 cups cooked white rice

Instructions:

1. In a Dutch oven or stockpot, sauté onions in butter.

2. Add diced tomatoes, tomato juice, water, chicken bouillon, and sugar. Simmer together for 30 minutes.

3. Add baking soda.

4. In a separate saucepan, heat half-and-half, cream, and milk. Add to soup. (Do not add cold milk to hot milk mixture or it might curdle.)

5. Add the rice and stir.

Note: For a creamier soup, blend the diced tomatoes before using.

There is nothing more comforting on a cold, snowy winter day than to have tomato soup simmering on the stove! I could "drink" this soup all day. —Emily

CHEESY ONION SOUP

Makes 4 servings

Ingredients:

2 cups thinly sliced sweet onions
6 tablespoons butter, *divided*
14 ½-ounce can chicken broth
2 teaspoons chicken bouillon
½ teaspoon pepper
3 tablespoons flour
1½ cups milk
¼ cup cubed Velveeta cheese

Instructions:

1. Cook onions in 3 tablespoons butter until onions are soft.

2. Add broth, bouillon, and pepper and bring to a boil.

3. In a large saucepan, melt remaining butter. Stir in flour until smooth.

4. Gradually add milk and bring to a boil. Cook and stir until thickened.

5. Reduce heat. Add cheese and onions. Cook and stir until heated through and cheese is melted.

My oldest sister serves this soup paired with one of her famous ham sandwiches at the farmers' market in Chambersburg, Pennsylvania. She always adds either a sharp cheddar cheese or Parmesan to give it an extra tasty, creamy base. —Emily

FRENCH ONION SOUP

Makes 4–6 servings

Ingredients:

3 medium sweet onions
2 tablespoons butter
3 cups water
3 cups beef stock
2 tablespoons beef bouillon
1 teaspoon salt
½ teaspoon pepper
2 cups croutons or cubed bread
1½ cups mozzarella cheese

Instructions:

1. In a Dutch oven or stockpot, sauté onions in butter until browned.

2. Add next five ingredients and bring to a boil. Simmer for 1 hour.

3. Pour soup into small oven-safe bowls or cups, then top with croutons and then cheese.

4. Broil until cheese is browned.

POTATO SOUP

Makes 4–6 servings

Ingredients:

4 medium uncooked potatoes, peeled and grated
1 medium carrot, peeled and grated
2 tablespoons diced onions
2½–3 cups water, *divided*
2–3 chicken bouillon cubes
1–2 teaspoons parsley
4 cups milk
2 tablespoons butter
2 tablespoons flour
½–1 cup water

Instructions:

1. Place potatoes, carrot, and onions in medium saucepan.

2. Add 2 cups water and chicken bouillon cubes.

3. Cook, covered, over medium-low heat until vegetables are tender. Stir frequently.

4. Add parsley, milk, and butter.

5. In separate bowl, combine flour and ½–1 cup water to make a paste. Blend together until smooth.

6. Stir flour paste into hot soup to thicken. Continue stirring over heat until soup broth becomes smooth and thickens.

When we were very small, my father owned a harness shop and times were lean. My parents were fun loving, so to go on a picnic with the horse and buggy was great. The larder was low, so Mam cooked a pot of this potato soup, wrapped it in a towel, and off we went. —Linda

STUFFED PEPPER SOUP

Makes 6–8 servings

Ingredients:
2 pounds ground beef
1 tablespoon chopped onion, *optional*
2 cups chopped green peppers
2 quarts water
28 ounces diced tomatoes
29 ounces tomato sauce
½ cup uncooked rice
2 teaspoons beef bouillon
2 teaspoons salt
¼ cup brown sugar
1 teaspoon pepper
½ teaspoon garlic pepper

Instructions:
1. In a Dutch oven or stockpot, brown beef, onion, and peppers.

2. Add remaining ingredients. Bring to a boil and then reduce heat and simmer for 30 minutes.

Note: You can add sliced mushrooms along with the onion and peppers.

TACO SOUP

Makes 6–8 servings

Ingredients:

½ teaspoon cumin
1 teaspoon chili powder
½ teaspoon oregano
½ teaspoon paprika
1 teaspoon salt
½ teaspoon pepper
1 tablespoon oil
1 pound beef
1 small onion
½ bell pepper
1½ cups diced tomatoes
16 ounces kidney beans, drained
1 cup corn
3 cloves garlic, minced
2 cups beef broth

Instructions:

1. Combine seasonings. Heat oil in a Dutch oven or stockpot, brown the beef, and add the seasonings.

2. Meanwhile, finely chop onion and pepper.

3. Once meat is browned, add remaining ingredients. Turn heat to low and cook 12–15 minutes.

RIVVEL SOUP

Makes 4 servings

Ingredients:

1 quart milk
2 tablespoons butter
1 cup flour
½ teaspoon salt
1 egg, well beaten
Salt and pepper to taste

Instructions:

1. In large saucepan, heat milk and butter until boiling.

2. In separate bowl, combine flour, salt, and egg. Mix with hands or table fork until small lumps appear.

3. Break off pieces, each about ½ inch round, known as "rivvels," and drop one by one into boiling milk.

4. Stir frequently to keep rivvels suspended in broth and to prevent them from clumping together.

5. When all rivvels are in soup, reduce heat to low and simmer 5 minutes.

6. Season with salt and pepper to taste.

Rivvel soup was one dish Mam made for Dat alone, the rest of us turning up our aristocratic noses. Somehow, those pale, misshapen rivvels seemed like raw dough. But Dat loved his rivvel soup. What did we eat on rivvel soup night? It may well have been cornflakes. Who knows? —Linda

COLD MILK SOUP

Makes 1 serving

Ingredients:
1 slice bread
1 cup fruit, fresh *or* canned
1 cup very cold milk
Sugar, *optional*

Instructions:
1. Crumble bread into bowl.
2. Pour fruit and milk over bread.
3. Sprinkle with sugar if you wish.
4. Multiply as many times as needed for the number of persons eating.

Note: This fast, usually summertime, soup is refreshing and filling. It's good for snacks and for when the cook is busy in the garden or canning the garden's bounty.

Cold Milk Soup is an acquired taste, definitely of Dutch origin. On hot summer days after working in the garden, then canning dozens of jars of vegetables, cold soup is a blessing. Strawberries, raspberries, cherries, peaches, bananas, or any fruit sugared liberally and poured over broken bread pieces with cold rich milk over all . . . delicious. —Linda

CHICKEN AND RICE SOUP

Makes 10 servings

Ingredients:

2 cups mixed vegetables such as celery, carrots, broccoli, and onion

1 cup cooked shredded chicken

2 quarts (8 cups) chicken broth

1 cup water

1 cup brown or white rice

1 teaspoon chicken seasoning or bouillon

Salt and pepper to taste

Instructions:

1. Wash and trim vegetables and place them in a powerful blender or food processor to finely chop. Transfer to the crock of a 6-quart slow cooker.

2. Add chicken, chicken broth, water, rice, and seasonings.

3. Cover and cook on low for 8–10 hours.

> When I think of chicken noodle soup, it takes me right back to my childhood. Mom taught school, so that left my oldest sister at home with me. Soup was on the menu for lunch almost every day. Still to this day, soup is one of my favorite things to make and eat! So comforting. —Emily

CHICKEN NOODLE SOUP

Serves 6–8

Ingredients:

3 quarts water
1 cup diced celery
2 cups diced carrots
½ cup diced onion
4 teaspoons chicken bouillon
2 teaspoons salt
½ teaspoon pepper
½ teaspoon basil
1 teaspoon dried parsley
1 pound chicken, chopped and precooked
8 ounces linguine pasta
¼ cup sour cream
14 cup water
1 tablespoon cornstarch

Instructions:

1. Heat water in a large pot. Add vegetables, seasonings, and chicken. Boil for 10 minutes.

2. Add pasta and boil for 10 more minutes, stirring occasionally.

3. Whisk together sour cream, water, and cornstarch.

4. While stirring soup, pour sour cream mixture into it. Reduce to simmer.

CHICKEN STEW

Makes 6–8 servings

Ingredients:

3 cups cooked chunks chicken
1 quart chicken broth
2 teaspoons granular chicken bouillon
2 cups cubed potatoes
2 cups peas
2 tablespoons chopped onion
2 cups sliced carrots
1 tablespoon parsley
1 teaspoon salt
Pepper to taste

Paste

3 tablespoons flour
1 cup water

Instructions:

1. Place first 10 ingredients in an 8-quart kettle.

2. Cover and bring to a boil.

3. Reduce heat and simmer until vegetables are soft.

4. To thicken stew, combine flour and water in separate bowl to make a paste. Stir until smooth.

5. Stir paste into stew to thicken. Continue stirring over low heat until smooth and thickened.

Tip: This stew is delicious served with dumplings on top (see Dumpling recipe on page 51) or with Potpie Noodles (see page 53).

Dad bought us a glossy new toboggan after about a foot of snow in January. After narrowly avoiding serious mishaps, we all stomped into the enclosed back porch, soaking wet, boots packed with snow. We sniffed the air and knew we had Chicken Stew and Dumplings for supper. We enjoyed it along with the ever-present applesauce, which we had made and canned from 10 bushels of apples (we made 200 quarts!). —Linda

DUMPLINGS TO GO WITH CHICKEN STEW

Makes 4–6 servings

Ingredients:

1½ cups sifted flour
3 teaspoons baking powder
¼ teaspoon salt
1 egg
½ cup milk

Instructions:

1. In medium bowl, combine flour, baking powder, and salt.

2. Add egg and stir until crumbly.

3. Slowly add milk until dough is sticky. Use only enough milk to moisten ingredients.

4. Drop dumpling batter by tablespoonfuls into simmering stew (after step 5 in Chicken Stew recipe on page 49).

5. Cook 10 minutes uncovered.

6. Cover. Cook 10 more minutes.

POTPIE NOODLES TO GO WITH CHICKEN STEW

Makes 6–8 servings

Ingredients:
2 cups flour
2 eggs
2–3 tablespoons milk, *or* cream
Chicken broth

Instructions:
1. Put flour in small bowl.
2. Add eggs and stir with fork until crumbly.
3. Add milk to make a soft dough.
4. Sprinkle additional flour on work area.
5. Place dough on floured surface and roll out as thin as possible.
6. Cut into 1-inch or 2-inch squares.
7. Drop into Chicken Stew's boiling broth. (See recipe for Chicken Stew on page 49.)
8. Cook for 20 minutes, or until noodles are tender.

BAKED BEEF STEW

Makes 6–8 servings

Ingredients:
2 pounds cubed stewing meat
1 cup V8 juice
6 carrots, sliced
3 medium potatoes, peeled and cubed
½ cup chopped celery
1 medium onion, sliced
3 tablespoons minute tapioca
1 slice bread, crumbled
1 cup water
2 tablespoons brown sugar
1 tablespoon Worcestershire sauce

Instructions:
1. In large bowl, combine all ingredients.
2. Mix well.
3. Pour into well-greased 3-quart baking dish.
4. Cover and bake at 325°F for 3 hours.

CHILI

Makes 6 servings

Ingredients:

1 pound beef
1 onion, chopped
1 bell pepper, chopped
2 tablespoons minced garlic
1 can black beans
1 can great northern beans
1 quart (4 cups) tomato juice
1 tablespoon white vinegar
1 tablespoon brown sugar
2 teaspoons chili powder
½ teaspoon cumin
¼ teaspoon paprika, *optional*
¼ teaspoon oregano
½ teaspoon pepper
½ teaspoon salt
1 teaspoon beef bouillon

Instructions:

1. In a large pot, brown the beef. Add onion and pepper and sauté until soft. Add garlic and sauté for 2 more minutes.

2. Add remaining ingredients and simmer on low for at least an hour.

Note: You can replace the tomato juice with V8. It gives it a really good tangy vegetable flavor. Delicious served with sour cream and/or shredded cheddar cheese.

Casseroles

BAKED CORN

Ingredients:

2 eggs

2 cups corn

1 cup milk

⅔ cup crushed cracker crumbs

3 tablespoons butter, melted

½ teaspoon salt

¼ teaspoon, *or* less, pepper

1 tablespoon sugar

¼ cup minced onion

Instructions:

1. Preheat oven to 350°F.

2. In a small bowl, beat eggs.

3. In a separate bowl, combine all other ingredients.

4. Add eggs and mix well.

5. Pour into 1½-quart greased casserole dish. Bake for 40–45 minutes, or until knife inserted in center of dish comes out clean.

Baked corn is the crowning glory of Pennsylvania Dutch cooking. Golden brown, loaded with savory corn kernels, oozing butter, puffed up like vanity itself when taken from the oven, filling the entire house with its rich aroma . . . it can't be beat. —Linda

BAKED CREAMED CORN

Makes 4–6 servings

Ingredients:
2 cups creamed corn
2 tablespoons sugar
1 cup milk
2 eggs
2 tablespoons flour
1 teaspoon salt
½ teaspoon pepper
2 tablespoons butter

Instructions:
1. Preheat oven to 350°F. Grease a 1½-quart casserole dish.

2. In a large mixing bowl, use a wooden spoon to beat all ingredients together.

3. Pour into casserole dish and bake for 1 hour.

GREEN BEAN CASSEROLE

Makes 6 servings

Ingredients:

2 (16-ounce) packages frozen green beans

10¾-ounce can cream of chicken, celery, *or* mushroom soup

½ cup milk

⅛ teaspoon pepper

1 (2.8-ounce) can French-fried onions, *optional*

Instructions:

1. Preheat oven to 350°F.

2. Cook green beans in small amount of water, covered, for approximately 10 minutes in saucepan. Drain. Green beans will be slightly crunchy.

3. In large bowl, mix soup, milk, and pepper together until smooth. Stir in beans.

4. Place mixture into greased 2- to 2½-quart baking dish.

5. Sprinkle with onions. Bake for 40 minutes.

POTLUCK POTATOES

Makes 10–12 servings

Ingredients:

2–3 pounds potatoes
¾ cup (1½ sticks) butter, *divided*
½ cup chopped onion
1 teaspoon salt
¼ teaspoon pepper
10¾-ounce can cream of chicken soup
1 pint sour cream
2 cups cubed Velveeta cheese
2 cups crushed cornflakes

Instructions:

1. Peel potatoes. Place in saucepan with about 2 inches of water.

2. Cover. Cook over medium heat until soft. Drain.

3. Allow potatoes to cool in fridge until completely cold, 5–6 hours, or overnight. (Cold potatoes shred far easier than those that aren't.)

4. Grease a 9×13 baking dish. Preheat oven to 350°F.

5. When potatoes are thoroughly cold, shred and place in greased baking dish.

6. In a small saucepan, combine ½ cup butter, onions, salt, pepper, soup, sour cream, and cheese.

7. Stirring occasionally, cook on medium heat until cheese is melted.

8. Pour cheese sauce over potatoes.

9. Bake for 15 minutes.

10. Melt remaining ¼ cup butter. Combine with crushed cornflakes.

11. Sprinkle cornflakes over potatoes and return to oven.

12. Bake 30–40 more minutes.

SCALLOPED POTATOES

Makes 10–12 servings

Ingredients:
8–10 medium potatoes
1 medium onion, chopped
4 tablespoons butter
2–3 cups milk
¾–1 teaspoon salt
¼ teaspoon pepper
1 cup water
1 tablespoon flour
1 cup shredded cheese of your choice

Instructions:
1. Peel potatoes and cook in enough water to cover over medium heat until medium soft, but allow for a little crunch.

2. Meanwhile, grease a 9×13 baking dish. Preheat oven to 350°F.

3. When potatoes are cool, slice into greased baking dish.

4. In medium saucepan, cook onion in butter until soft.

5. Add milk to onions.

6. Add salt and pepper.

7. In a separate bowl, stir water and flour into a smooth paste.

8. Add flour mixture to onion mixture. Over medium heat, stir continually until sauce becomes creamy and thickened.

9. Remove from heat and stir in cheese until melted.

10. Pour sauce over potatoes and mix together.

11. Bake for 1 hour.

SWEET POTATO CASSEROLE

Makes 6 servings

Ingredients:

3 medium to large sweet potatoes, peeled
2 eggs
½ cup milk
¼ cup sugar
½ teaspoon salt
4 tablespoons butter, melted
½ teaspoon vanilla

Crumbs

½ cup sugar
1 cup chopped nuts
⅓ cup flour
3 tablespoons butter, melted

Instructions:

1. Cook potatoes in saucepan in about 2 inches water, covered, until very tender.

2. Drain potatoes. Mash until smooth.

3. Preheat oven to 350°F.

4. In large mixing bowl mix together eggs, milk, sugar, salt, butter, and vanilla.

5. Stir potatoes into egg mixture.

6. Spoon into greased 2-quart baking dish.

7. To make crumbs, combine sugar, nuts, flour, and butter in a small bowl.

8. Sprinkle crumbs over potatoes.

9. Bake for 35–45 minutes, or until heated through.

ZUCCHINI CASSEROLE

Makes 6–8 servings

Ingredients:

3 eggs

¼ cup vegetable oil

½ cup flour

½ teaspoon salt

1½ teaspoons baking powder

½ cup grated cheese of your choice

¼ cup parsley

½ cup chopped onion

2 cups unpeeled grated zucchini

Instructions:

1. Preheat oven to 350°F.

2. In medium bowl, beat eggs and oil together.

3. Stir in flour, salt, and baking powder.

4. Add cheese, parsley, onion, and zucchini. Mix well.

5. Pour into greased 2-quart casserole dish. Bake for 45 minutes.

BROCCOLI CASSEROLE

Makes 10–12 servings

Ingredients:
2 (10-ounce) packages frozen chopped broccoli
2 eggs, beaten
1 cup mayonnaise
1 can cream of mushroom soup
¼ cup chopped onion
3½ cups sharp cheddar cheese, divided
Salt and pepper
½ cup bread crumbs or cracker crumbs

Instructions:
1. Preheat oven to 350°F.

2. Cook broccoli, drain, and cool.

3. Combine broccoli, eggs, mayonnaise, soup, onion, and 2 cups of the cheese.

4. Add salt and pepper.

5. In a 9×13 pan, bake 30 minutes and then sprinkle with crumbs, top with remaining cheese, and bake 10 minutes longer.

MASHED POTATO CASSEROLE

Makes 6–8 servings

Ingredients:

6–7 large potatoes, peeled, cut, and cooked until soft
½ cup milk
1 (8-ounce) package cream cheese
1 cup sour cream
1 teaspoon garlic salt
Salt and pepper to taste
1 cup shredded cheddar cheese
Bacon crumbles
Chives

Instructions:

1. Preheat oven to 350°F.

2. Drain potatoes and mash or mix until smooth.

3. Mix in all other ingredients except cheese, bacon, and chives.

4. Transfer to a 9×13 pan. Put cheese on top and cover with foil. Bake for 30 minutes, then uncover, add bacon and chives, and bake a bit longer.

AMISH WEDDING COOKED CELERY

Makes about 15 servings

Ingredients:
12 quarts chopped celery
2 cups sugar
¼ pound butter
1 cup water

Paste
3 tablespoons flour
1 cup brown sugar
1 cup sugar
1 cup evaporated milk
2 tablespoons vinegar

Instructions:

1. In a 12-quart pot, combine celery, sugar, butter, and water and cook until celery is soft.

2. In a bowl, combine the paste ingredients and then slowly add to the celery mixture. Do not boil. Simmer for 1 hour.

BREAKFAST CASSEROLE

Makes 6–8 servings

Ingredients:

6–8 medium potatoes, peeled *or* unpeeled

8 eggs

2 teaspoons water

¾ teaspoons salt

¼ teaspoon pepper

3 cups sharp cheese, grated

Instructions:

1. Cook potatoes until medium-soft. They should still be slightly crunchy. Cool to room temperature.

2. Refrigerate for 2 hours to make shredding easier.

3. After chilling, preheat oven to 350°F. Shred potatoes and place in the bottom of a greased 9×13 baking dish.

4. In separate bowl, beat eggs, water, salt, and pepper together.

5. Pour egg mixture over potatoes and sprinkle with cheese.

6. Bake for 30 minutes, covered. Take off cover and continue baking for 15 minutes.

7. Let stand 10 minutes before serving.

Variations:

1. Add more vegetables by adding green peppers or onion to the egg mixture in step 4.
2. Sprinkle cooked ham, bacon, or sausage over mixture before adding cheese in step 5.

CHEESY BREAKFAST CASSEROLE

Makes 8–10 servings

Ingredients:

Cheese Sauce

2 tablespoons butter
2 tablespoons flour
2 cups milk
½ teaspoon salt
⅛ teaspoon pepper
13 slices American cheese

Egg Mixture

¼ cup chopped onion
3 tablespoons butter
1 dozen eggs
1 cup ham, sausage, or bacon

Topping

½ cup butter, melted
4 ½ cups (8 slices) bread cubes

Instructions:

1. Preheat oven to 350°F. Grease a 9×13 baking pan.

2. To make the cheese sauce, melt butter in a medium saucepan.

3. Whisk in the flour until incorporated, then add milk, salt, and pepper. Continue stirring with whisk until hot.

4. Add cheese and cook and stir until fully melted. Turn off heat and set aside.

5. To make the egg mixture, sauté the onion in 3 tablespoons butter. Add eggs and meat and scramble eggs until cooked through.

6. Pour egg mixture into greased pan. Pour cheese sauce over top.

7. To make the topping, mix together the melted butter and bread cubes. Spread over the top of the casserole.

8. Bake until hot and bread cubes are lightly toasted.

COUNTRY BRUNCH

Makes 10–12 servings

Ingredients:
16 slices bread
3 cups cubed ham
2 pounds cheese of your choice (muenster works well)
3 cups milk
6 eggs
½ cup butter
3 cups cornflakes

Instructions:

1. Preheat oven to 375°F. Grease the bottom of a 9×13 baking dish.

2. Divide the bread, ham, and cheese in half and create two layers of each (bread, ham, cheese, bread, ham, cheese).

3. Beat together the milk and eggs and pour over the casserole.

4. Refrigerate overnight.

5. In the morning, melt the butter. Add the cornflakes to the butter and mix. Pour over casserole.

6. Bake for 45 minutes.

BAKED FRENCH TOAST

Makes 6–8 servings

Ingredients:

3 tablespoons butter
⅓ cup brown sugar
Cinnamon to taste
6 slices bread
6 eggs
1 cup milk

Instructions:

1. Melt butter and pour into bottom of 9×13 baking pan.

2. Sprinkle brown sugar and cinnamon on top of butter.

3. Layer bread slices on top of sugar and cinnamon.

4. In separate bowl, beat eggs.

5. Add milk and beat well.

6. Pour over bread slices.

7. Refrigerate for 8 hours, or overnight.

8. Bake at 350°F for 35–45 minutes, or until browned.

The first time I tasted Baked French Toast, I knew my beloved pancakes had been upstaged. Crispy, doughy, gooey, and sweet, with syrup an added luxury, it's almost too much. I could write a love song to a fresh pan of French Toast taken from the oven. —Linda

BAKED OATMEAL

Makes 6 servings

Ingredients:
½ cup (1 stick) butter, melted
1 cup brown sugar
2 eggs, beaten
3 cups quick oats
1 cup milk
2 teaspoons baking powder
1 teaspoon salt

Instructions:

1. Preheat oven to 350°F.

2. Combine melted butter, brown sugar, and eggs.

3. Stir in remaining ingredients and mix well.

4. Pour into well-greased 8×8 casserole or baking dish.

5. Bake for 30 minutes.

6. Serve, hot, cold, or at room temperature with milk.

CHICKEN PIE

Makes 4 pies

Ingredients:

3 tablespoons butter
4 ribs celery, chopped
4 medium carrots, chopped
1 large onion, chopped
¼ cup flour
1 teaspoon salt
1 cup milk
1 cup chicken broth
10¾-oz. can cream of mushroom soup
4 cups cooked, cut-up chicken
4 (9-inch) unbaked piecrusts, plus dough for 4 top crusts (see page 92)

Instructions:

1. Preheat oven to 350°F.

2. In large skillet, melt butter. Add vegetables and cook until soft.

3. Stir in flour and salt.

4. Slowly add milk and broth, stirring constantly.

5. Cook until sauce thickens.

6. Remove from heat and stir in soup.

7. Stir in chicken.

8. Pour into prepared piecrusts and top with pastry top.

9. Bake for 35–45 minutes.

PIECRUST

Makes 2 (9-inch) double-crust pies

Ingredients:

4 cups flour
1 teaspoon salt
1 teaspoon baking powder
1 tablespoon sugar
2 cups shortening (Crisco works well)
¼–⅓ cup water

Instructions:

1. In a large bowl, combine flour, salt, baking powder, and sugar.

2. Use a fork, a pastry cutter, or 2 table knives to cut in shortening.

3. When mixture is crumbly and resembles small peas, add water, a few tablespoons at a time. Stir in water with a fork, using just enough water, until the pastry forms a ball.

4. Using your hands, divide dough into 4 equal amounts.

5. Sprinkle work area with flour.

6. Roll out one ball of dough with a rolling pin.

7. Rolling away from yourself, make a circular piecrust about ⅛ inch thick and 2 inches bigger than the pie plate.

8. When the crust is the right size, loosely fold the dough in half and place into pie plate. Open up to fill plate. Press firmly in place with your fingers.

9. Using a table knife, trim off the extra edges of the crust.

10. Fill the pie with desired pie filling.

11. To make a top crust, roll out a second ball of dough.

12. Rolling away from yourself, make a circular piecrust that is slightly thinner than the bottom crust and about 1 inch bigger than the pie plate.

13. Cut about 6 slits in this top dough crust, spacing the slits evenly, to allow steam to escape when the pie is baking.

14. Using a pastry brush or your fingers, moisten the edges of the bottom piecrust with cold water.

15. Place dough top carefully over pie filling.

16. Using your fingertips, press top and bottom edges together to seal.

17. Moving around the pie, pinch the edges into a V-shape to form fluting, or press firmly with tines of a fork.

18. Bake according to pie recipe.

19. Repeat this process with the other 2 balls of dough.

QUICK AND EASY CHICKEN PIE

Makes 4 servings

Ingredients:

2 cups cooked mixed vegetables

1 cup cooked and diced chicken

10¾-ounce can cream of chicken soup

1 cup buttermilk baking mix

½ cup milk

1 egg

Instructions:

1. Preheat oven to 400°F.

2. In medium bowl, combine vegetables, chicken, and soup.

3. Pour mixture into 2-quart greased baking dish or 10-inch pie plate.

4. In separate bowl, stir together baking mix, milk, and egg.

5. Drop by tablespoonfuls over vegetable-chicken mixture.

6. Bake for 30 minutes.

CHICKEN CASSEROLE

Makes 6–8 servings

Ingredients:

1 cup (2 sticks) butter, *divided*
6 cups soft bread cubes
¼ cup minced onion
1 teaspoon celery salt
½ teaspoon salt
¼ cup flour
½ cup milk
1 cup chicken broth
3 cups cooked and chopped chicken
2 cups cooked peas, *or* green beans

Instructions:

1. Preheat oven to 375°F.

2. Melt ½ cup (1 stick) butter.

3. In large bowl, combine melted butter, bread cubes, onion, celery salt, and salt.

4. Pour into greased 9×13 baking dish and bake for 15 minutes.

5. Meanwhile, in large saucepan, melt other stick of butter.

6. Stir in flour.

7. Stirring constantly over medium heat, add milk and broth.

8. Continuing to stir, cook until thickened.

9. Stir in chicken and peas.

10. Pour mixture over bread cubes and continue baking for 20–30 minutes.

POTATO AND CHICKEN CASSEROLE

Makes 10–12 servings

Ingredients:

9x13 pan half full of shredded potatoes or tater tots
6 chicken breasts, cooked and cubed
2 cups diced carrots and peas (frozen is ok)
1 small onion, chopped
½ cup butter
8 ounces cream cheese
12 ounces grated cheddar cheese
1 can cream of chicken soup
1 teaspoon salt

Topping

2 cups crushed cornflakes
½ cup butter, melted

Instructions:

1. Preheat oven to 325°F.

2. Lay chicken on top of potatoes. Add carrots and peas.

3. Sauté onions in butter until translucent.

4. Add cheeses, soup, and salt. Heat, stirring occasionally.

5. Pour mixture over chicken and potatoes.

6. Mix together the cornflakes and butter and distribute evenly over top of the casserole just before baking.

7. Bake for 1 hour.

CHICKEN NOODLE BAKE

Makes 6–8 servings

Ingredients:
8-ounce package elbow noodles
4 tablespoons butter
3 tablespoons flour
2 cups milk
¼ cup chopped onion
1 teaspoon salt
⅛ teaspoon pepper
2½ cups shredded cheese
2 cups cooked and chopped chicken

Instructions:

1. Cook noodles according to directions on package. Drain noodles.

2. Preheat oven to 350°F.

3. In a separate saucepan, melt butter.

4. Add flour and cook for 2 minutes, stirring constantly. Do not brown.

5. Continue to stir and slowly pour in milk.

6. Add onion, salt, and pepper and cook over medium heat until thickened, stirring continually.

7. Remove from heat and stir in cheese.

8. Mix cheese sauce, noodles, and chicken together in a large bowl.

9. Pour into greased 9×13 baking dish and bake for 30 minutes.

CHICKEN GUMBO

Makes 10–12 servings

Ingredients:

9 slices bread, toasted and cubed
4 cups cooked and cubed chicken
4 tablespoons butter, melted
½ cup Miracle Whip salad dressing
4 eggs, beaten
1 cup chicken broth
1 cup milk
1 teaspoon salt
2 (10¾-ounce) cans cream of celery soup
9 slices cheese of your choice

Instructions:

1. Preheat oven to 350°F.

2. Place bread cubes on bottom of greased 9×13 baking dish.

3. Sprinkle chicken over top.

4. In separate bowl, combine melted butter, Miracle Whip, eggs, broth, milk, salt, and soup.

5. Pour mixture over chicken.

6. Top with cheese.

7. Bake for 30–45 minutes, or until lightly browned.

GRANDMA K'S ASIAN CHICKEN

Ingredients:

2 pounds chicken legs or thighs
All-purpose flour
Sprinkle garlic salt
Sprinkle seasoned salt
Sprinkle paprika
Oil for frying

Sauce

1 cup sugar
½ cup vinegar
1½ cups water
1½ tablespoons soy sauce
½ teaspoon salt
2 or 3 tablespoons cornstarch or flour

Instructions:

1. Dip chicken pieces in flour and then sprinkle with garlic salt, seasoned salt, and paprika.

2. Fry chicken in oil until golden brown. Place fried chicken in a casserole dish.

3. Preheat oven to 350°F.

4. In a medium saucepan, combine sauce ingredients and bring to a boil. Pour over fried chicken and bake for 1½ hours.

ROASHT OR CHICKEN FILLING

Makes 15 servings

Ingredients:
½ cup (1 stick) butter
2 cups chopped celery
2 loaves bread, cubed
3 cups cooked and diced chicken
6 eggs, beaten
1 teaspoon salt
Pepper to taste

Instructions:

1. Preheat oven to 350°F.

2. Melt butter in large skillet.

3. Add celery and sauté until soft.

4. Toss bread and chicken together in a large bowl.

5. Pour celery and eggs over bread mixture.

6. Sprinkle with salt and pepper and mix well.

7. Pour into greased roaster or large baking dish.

8. Bake uncovered at 350°F for 1½–2 hours.

9. During baking time, stir occasionally, stirring bread away from sides of pan to prevent burning.

OHIO FILLING

Makes 15 servings

Ingredients:

1 cup chopped celery
½ cup diced potatoes
½–1 cup chopped carrots
2 loaves bread, cubed
1 cup (2 sticks) butter, melted
6 eggs, beaten
5–6 cups milk
1 cup chicken broth
1 tablespoon chicken bouillon
½ teaspoon pepper
1 teaspoon seasoned salt
2 tablespoons parsley, fresh *or* dried
2 cups cooked and diced chicken

My mother was born and raised in Holmes County, Ohio, where the customs and traditions are different than here in the East. She always looked down her nose at our Roascht, or Chicken Filling, saying it wasn't very good. Her version of a holiday or wedding meal was Ohio Filling with fried chicken. She called the filling "dressing" and it had toasted bread cubes, carrots, potatoes and celery, loads of butter, eggs, and chicken broth. She clung to this western dressing and fried chicken all her life. —Linda

Instructions:

1. In saucepan, cook celery, potatoes, and carrots over medium heat, in about 1 inch of water, until tender.

2. In large bowl, toss bread cubes with melted butter.

3. Spread bread cubes onto 2 baking sheets.

4. Toast at 375°F in oven for 20 minutes, or until nicely browned.

5. In large mixing bowl, combine eggs, milk, broth, bouillon, pepper, seasoned salt, and parsley.

6. Add chicken, celery, potatoes, carrots, and toasted bread cubes. Mix together gently.

7. Pour into large greased roaster or 1 or 2 baking pans.

8. Bake uncovered at 350°F for 1½–2 hours.

9. Stir occasionally.

10. Serve when top is brown and crusty.

TURKEY BAKE

Makes 6–8 servings

Ingredients:

8 slices bread, cubed, *divided*

2 cups cooked, cubed turkey

2 cups shredded cheese

¼ cup chopped onion

1 tablespoon butter

2 cups milk

3 eggs

½ teaspoon salt

¼ teaspoon pepper

Instructions:

1. Preheat oven to 350°F.

2. Place half of bread cubes in well-greased 9×9 baking pan or casserole dish.

3. Spread turkey over bread.

4. Sprinkle cheese over turkey.

5. In a small skillet, sauté onion in butter.

6. Spread onion over cheese.

7. Cover with remaining bread cubes.

8. In separate bowl, stir milk, eggs, salt, and pepper together. Pour over casserole.

9. Bake for 40 minutes.

Note: This casserole is almost a quick version of "roasht" (see page 107).

Turkey Bake was a good way to use leftover Thanksgiving turkey, if we were lucky enough to have one. Fragrant bits of turkey assured us of another tasty meat dish, even if there was more filler than actual turkey.
—Linda

TATER TOT CASSEROLE

Makes 10 servings

Ingredients:

1 large onion
3 pounds ground beef
Salt and pepper to taste
1 bag peas
2 cans cream of mushroom soup
1 bag Tater Tots
2 cups grated cheddar cheese

Instructions:

1. Preheat oven to 350°F.

2. In a large frying pan, sauté onion and ground beef, stirring frequently, until onions are soft and ground beef is browned. Transfer to the bottom of a 9×13 pan.

3. Sprinkle meat with salt and pepper. Place peas evenly on top of ground beef.

4. Spread mushroom soup over peas and place the Tater Tots on top of the mushroom soup.

5. Cover with cheese and bake, covered with foil, for 1 hour.

BEEF AND POTATO LOAF

Makes 4–6 servings

Ingredients:
4 cups raw potatoes
1 tablespoon chopped onion
1 teaspoon salt

Meat Loaf
1 pound ground beef
¾ cup milk
½ cup dry oatmeal, quick *or* rolled
¼ cup ketchup
¼ cup diced onion
1 teaspoon salt
¼ teaspoon pepper

Instructions:

1. Preheat oven to 350°F.

2. Peel potatoes and slice very thin.

3. Place potatoes, onion, and salt into bottom of greased 3-quart casserole dish.

4. Mix together meat loaf ingredients. Shape into loaf.

5. Place meat loaf on top of potatoes.

6. Bake for 1–1½ hours, or until potatoes are soft.

7. If meat loaf begins to get too dark while baking, cover with foil.

Tip: Spread additional ketchup over top of meat loaf before baking, if you wish.

MEAT LOAF

Makes 8 servings

Ingredients:

Meat Loaf

1½ pounds ground beef

¾ cup dry quick oats

1 egg, beaten

¾ cup milk

1½ teaspoons salt

¼ cup chopped onion

¼ teaspoon pepper

Sauce

½ cup ketchup

2 tablespoons brown sugar

1 tablespoon prepared mustard

Instructions:

1. Preheat oven to 350°F.

2. Combine meat loaf ingredients in the order given.

3. With clean hands, mix well. Shape into loaf.

4. Place in well-greased pan.

5. Combine sauce ingredients and pour on top.

6. Bake for 1 hour.

CHEESE AND VEGGIE MEAT LOAF

Makes 6 servings

Ingredients:

2 eggs

⅔ cup milk

3 slices bread, cubed

½ cup chopped onion

½ cup grated carrots

I cup shredded cheddar or mozzarella cheese

I tablespoon chopped fresh parsley

I teaspoon dried parsley

I teaspoon dried basil, thyme, or sage (optional)

I teaspoon salt

¼ teaspoon pepper

I½ pounds ground beef

Topping

½ cup tomato sauce or ketchup

½ cup brown sugar

I teaspoon mustard

Instructions:

1. Preheat oven to 350°F.

2. In a large bowl, beat eggs. Add milk and bread and set aside until bread absorbs the liquid.

3. Stir in onion, carrots, cheese, herbs, salt, and pepper. Add beef and mix well.

4. In a shallow baking pan, shape beef into a 7×3×2-inch loaf. Bake for 45 minutes.

5. Combine topping ingredients.

6. Spoon half of topping onto meatloaf. Bake 30 minutes more, occasionally spooning some of the remaining topping over the loaf.

HOT ROAST HAMBURGER

Makes 6–8 servings

Ingredients:

1 pound ground beef

⅔ cup tomato juice

½ cup dry bread crumbs

¼ cup ketchup

1 teaspoon salt

2 teaspoons Worcestershire sauce

¼ teaspoon pepper

6–8 medium potatoes, sliced ½–¾-inch thick

4–6 medium carrots, sliced

1 large onion, sliced

Parsley

Salt and pepper to taste

Instructions:

1. Preheat oven to 300°F.

2. In large bowl, combine ground beef, tomato juice, bread crumbs, ketchup, salt, Worcestershire sauce, and pepper. Mix well and shape into loaf.

3. Place into a large, greased casserole dish or roaster.

4. Add potatoes, carrots, and onion in layers around meat loaf.

5. Sprinkle with parsley, salt, and pepper.

6. Bake for 2–3 hours, or at 375°F for 1–1½ hours.

HAMBURGER CASSEROLE

Makes 8–10 servings

Ingredients:

2 pounds ground beef

1 small onion, chopped

3 teaspoons salt, *divided*

2 (10¾-ounce) cans tomato soup

1½ quarts home-canned *or* 3 (15½-ounce) cans, green beans

9 medium potatoes

1 egg

¼ teaspoon pepper

½ cup warm milk

4 tablespoons butter, *optional*

Instructions:

1. Brown ground beef, onion, and 2 teaspoons salt in skillet until cooked and crumbly.

2. Drain off drippings.

3. In large bowl, combine ground beef, tomato soup, and green beans.

4. Pour into greased 9×13 baking dish. Preheat oven to 350°F.

5. Peel, cook, and mash potatoes.

6. When potatoes are mashed, add egg, 1 teaspoon salt, pepper, milk, and butter if you wish.

7. Spread potatoes over ground beef mixture.

8. Bake for 30–35 minutes.

MACARONI AND HAMBURGER CASSEROLE

Makes 6–8 servings

Ingredients:

1½ cups uncooked macaroni

2 teaspoons salt

1½ quarts water

2 tablespoons butter

¼ cup minced onion

1 pound ground beef

2 teaspoons flour

1 cup chopped green bell pepper

15½-ounce can diced tomatoes, undrained

½–1 cup grated cheese of your choice

Instructions:

1. Cook macaroni in salted water until tender.

2. Drain and set aside.

3. Preheat oven to 350°F.

4. Melt butter in medium skillet.

5. Fry onion and ground beef in butter until ground beef is brown and crumbly.

6. Stir in flour, pepper, and tomatoes.

7. Combine ground beef mixture and macaroni.

8. Pour into greased casserole dish.

9. Sprinkle with cheese.

10. Bake for 25 minutes.

PIZZA CASSEROLE

Makes 8–10 servings

Ingredients:

1 pound ground beef
¼ cup chopped onion
8-ounce. package elbow noodles or ziti
10¾-ounce can cream of mushroom soup
15-ounce jar pizza sauce
Pepperoni, *optional*
Chopped green bell peppers, *optional*
2 cups shredded mozzarella cheese

Instructions:

1. Brown ground beef in medium skillet. Stir frequently to break up clumps.

2. Add onion. Continue cooking until tender.

3. In separate pan, cook noodles until soft. Drain.

4. Preheat oven to 350°F.

5. Stir together ground beef and noodles in large mixing bowl.

6. Pour soup and pizza sauce over ground beef mixture and stir to combine.

7. Pour into greased 3-quart baking dish.

8. Top with pepperoni and peppers if you wish.

9. Sprinkle with cheese.

10. Bake for 35 minutes.

POOR MAN'S STEAK

Makes 4–5 servings

Ingredients:

1 pound ground beef
1 cup cracker crumbs, *or* dry oatmeal
1 small onion, chopped
1 teaspoon salt
¼ teaspoon pepper
1 cup milk
2 tablespoons butter
10¾-ounce can cream of mushroom soup

Instructions:

1. In large bowl, mix ground beef, cracker crumbs, onion, salt, pepper, and milk together.

2. Shape into loaf. Refrigerate 8–10 hours, or overnight.

3. Remove from refrigerator and slice into ½-inch-thick slices.

4. Preheat oven to 350°F.

5. Brown each slice in butter in skillet.

6. Place browned slices in greased 9×13 baking pan.

7. Cover with soup.

8. Bake, covered, for 45 minutes.

POUR PIZZA

Makes 8–10 servings

Ingredients:

1 pound ground beef
1 small onion, chopped
1 teaspoon salt
¼ teaspoon pepper
1 cup flour
2 eggs
⅔ cup milk
⅛–¼ teaspoon dried oregano
1–2 cups shredded cheese

Instructions:

1. In medium skillet, brown ground beef, onion, salt, and pepper together.

2. Preheat oven to 350°F.

3. In separate bowl, combine flour, eggs, milk, and oregano to create a batter.

4. Pour batter into well-greased 7×11 baking dish.

5. Top with ground beef mixture.

6. Bake for 15–20 minutes.

7. Remove from oven and sprinkle with cheese.

8. Return to oven for 15 minutes more.

Tip: Pour Pizza may be served with warmed spaghetti/pizza sauce for dipping.

SPAGHETTI PIZZA

Makes 10 servings

Ingredients:

1 pound spaghetti, cooked and drained
1 egg, beaten
⅓ cup milk
4 tablespoons butter, melted
2½ cups mozzarella cheese, *divided*
Spaghetti sauce
¼ cup Parmesan cheese
Pepperoni slices
Mushrooms (optional)

Instructions:

1. Preheat oven to 350°F.

2. Combine first 4 ingredients with ½ cup mozzarella cheese. Mix well.

3. Place in a greased 10½×15 baking pan with a cover (or use foil). Spread a thin layer of spaghetti sauce over top.

4. Add Parmesan cheese, remaining mozzarella cheese, pepperoni, and mushrooms (if using).

5. Bake, covered, for 35–40 minutes or until bubbly.

BARBECUED HAM SLICES

Makes 12–16 servings

Ingredients:

1 tablespoon butter
¼ cup chopped onion
½ cup ketchup
⅓ cup water
2 tablespoons brown sugar
1 tablespoon Worcestershire sauce
2 tablespoons white vinegar
12 slices boneless ham

Instructions:

1. Melt butter in medium saucepan.

2. Add onion and cook until soft.

3. Preheat oven to 350°F.

4. In a bowl, combine ketchup, water, brown sugar, Worcestershire sauce, and vinegar.

5. Add to saucepan with onion and bring to a boil. Simmer for 5 minutes.

6. Arrange ham slices in a single layer in large greased casserole dish (or dishes) or roaster. Pour sauce over ham.

7. Bake for 1½ hours. Baste occasionally with sauce.

HAM LOAF

Makes 8–10 servings

Ingredients:

Ham Loaf

1 pound ground ham
1 pound bulk sausage
2 cups soft bread crumbs
2 eggs, beaten
1 cup sour cream
1 teaspoon dry mustard
⅛ teaspoon paprika
⅛ teaspoon black pepper

Sauce

½ cup packed brown sugar
½ cup pineapple juice
1 tablespoon Clear Jel, or cornstarch

Instructions:

1. Preheat oven to 350°F.

2. In large bowl, mix together all ham loaf ingredients.

3. Form into a loaf and place in greased loaf pan.

4. Bake uncovered for 1 hour.

5. While ham loaf is baking, prepare sauce.

6. Combine ingredients for sauce in small pan.

7. Bring to a boil. Stir frequently over medium heat until smooth and thickened.

8. When ham loaf has baked for an hour, remove from oven.

9. Drain ham loaf drippings into prepared sauce.

10. Baste ham loaf with sauce.

11. Return to oven and bake 30 more minutes, or until lightly browned.

FARMERS' MARKET FARE

Makes about 10 servings

Ingredients:
2 medium potatoes
2 sweet potatoes
3 carrots
½ onion
2 tablespoons olive oil
1 teaspoon garlic salt
½ teaspoon pepper
1 teaspoon chicken seasoning
1 pound ground sausage or links *or*
   1 beef chuck roast

Instructions:

1. Preheat oven to 350°F.

2. Grease bottom and sides of a 9×13 pan.

3. Wash, peel, and dice potatoes, carrots, and onion. Drizzle with oil and sprinkle with seasonings.

4. Break up uncooked sausage *or* cut roast into bite-size pieces.

5. Combine everything in the pan.

6. Cover casserole tightly with lid or tinfoil and bake for 1 hour. Uncover and bake 10 more minutes.

GREEN BEAN AND SAUSAGE CASSEROLE

Makes 6–8 servings

Ingredients:

1–1½ pounds sausage, bulk *or* link

1 quart home-canned, *or* 2 (15½-ounce) cans, green beans

6 medium potatoes

¾ cup water

¼ pound grated cheddar cheese

10¾-ounce can cream of mushroom soup

Instructions:

1. Brown sausage in skillet, stirring frequently to break up clumps until no pink remains. Drain off drippings. Place sausage in large mixing bowl.

2. Drain green beans. Add to mixing bowl with meat.

3. Preheat oven to 350°F.

4. Peel and cut potatoes into cubes. Place cubed potatoes in saucepan with ¾ cup water.

5. Cover. Cook over low to medium heat until tender. Stir frequently to prevent sticking. Add more water if needed so potatoes don't cook dry.

6. When fully cooked, drain and add to meat and green beans in bowl. Stir together well.

7. Pour into greased 9×13 baking dish.

8. Add cheese and soup. Stir to combine.

9. Bake for 30 minutes.

SAUSAGE POTATO CASSEROLE

Makes 8–10 servings

Ingredients:

1 pound bulk pork sausage, *divided*

10¾-ounce can cream of mushroom soup

¾ cup milk

¼ cup chopped onion

½ teaspoon salt

½ teaspoon pepper

½ teaspoon parsley

3 cups raw potatoes, sliced thinly, *divided*

1 cup shredded cheese

Instructions:

1. In a large skillet, brown sausage. Stir frequently to break up clumps and until no pink remains. Drain off drippings.

2. Preheat oven to 350°F.

3. In separate bowl, mix together soup, milk, onion, and seasonings.

4. In a casserole dish, layer half the potatoes, then sausage, then soup mixture.

5. Repeat layers until ingredients are all used.

6. Cover and bake until potatoes are tender, about 60–70 minutes.

7. Remove from oven and sprinkle with cheese.

8. Return to oven, uncovered, until cheese is melted, about 10 more minutes.

ONE-POT SAUSAGE DISH

Makes 6–8 servings

Ingredients:

3 medium potatoes, cut into small chunks
2 cups medium pasta shells
Seasoned salt
I cup peas
3 sausage links, cooked and cut into bite-sized
  chunks
6–8 slices yellow American cheese
¼ cup butter

Instructions:

1. Arrange potato chunks and pasta shells in a skillet. Cover with water and cook until soft, sprinkling with seasoned salt.

2. When potatoes are soft, drain most of the water, leaving just a little in the skillet. Add peas and cooked sausage. Mix everything gently together over medium heat.

3. Cover with yellow American cheese slices and turn the burner off.

4. In a separate light-colored skillet, melt butter and stir constantly until light brown (about 5 minutes). Pour over cheese. Serve hot.

NOODLE AND SALMON CASSEROLE

Makes 10 servings

Ingredients:

2 tablespoons butter

1½ tablespoons flour

½ teaspoon pepper

1 cup milk

1 cup peas, drained, liquid reserved

4 cups cooked noodles

2 cups canned salmon, drained, liquid reserved

¼ cup cracker crumbs

Instructions:

1. Preheat oven to 350°F.

2. In a medium saucepan, melt butter. Stir in flour. Add pepper, milk, and liquid from peas and salmon and cook until thick.

3. Mix noodles, peas, and salmon in a greased 9×13 baking pan.

4. Pour sauce over noodles and top with cracker crumbs.

5. Bake for 25 minutes.

BAKED MACARONI AND CHEESE

Makes 6 servings

Ingredients:

1½ cups uncooked macaroni
5 tablespoons butter, *divided*
3 tablespoons flour
1½ cups milk
1 cup shredded cheddar cheese
½ cup cubed American cheese
½ teaspoon salt
¼ teaspoon pepper
2 tablespoons dried bread crumbs

Instructions:

1. Cook macaroni according to directions on package.

2. Drain and put in greased 2-quart baking dish.

3. Preheat oven to 350°F.

4. In medium saucepan, melt 4 tablespoons butter. Add flour and stir until smooth.

5. Stirring constantly, slowly pour in milk.

6. Boil for 2 minutes, stirring continually. Reduce heat to medium.

7. Stir in cheeses, salt, and pepper.

8. Pour over macaroni and mix well.

9. In separate saucepan, melt remaining butter.

10. Add bread crumbs and brown lightly.

11. Sprinkle bread crumbs over macaroni.

12. Bake uncovered for 30 minutes.

FLOATING ISLANDS

Makes 6–8 servings

Ingredients:
1 pound hot dogs
6 cups mashed potatoes
½–¾ pound cheese, cut in long, narrow strips
Sauerkraut, *optional*

Instructions:

1. Preheat oven to 350°F.

2. Heat hot dogs in saucepan on stovetop until warm in center.

3. Remove from pan and cut a slit down the length of each hot dog.

4. Fill with mashed potatoes.

5. Place cheese on top of potatoes.

6. Place hot dogs on cookie sheet or jelly-roll pan.

7. Bake for 20–30 minutes, or until well browned.

Variation: Sauerkraut goes well with Floating Islands. Heat the sauerkraut in a separate saucepan.

Breads & Rolls

BECKY ZOOK BREAD

Makes 5 loaves

Ingredients:

4 cups warm (110–112°F) water, *divided*
½ tablespoon dry, active yeast
½ cup and ½ tablespoons sugar, *divided*
¼ cup lard, *or* Crisco, melted
1 tablespoon salt
3 quarts Occident* flour

* Occident flour is bread flour made from western wheat.

Tip: To check if the bread is finished, tap the top. Bread is ready when you hear a dull sound.

Instructions:

1. In a small bowl, combine 1 cup warm water, yeast, and ½ tablespoon sugar. Stir and let stand until bubbly, approximately 2–5 minutes.

2. In another large bowl, mix 3 cups water, ½ cup sugar, lard, and salt.

3. Pour yeast mixture into the large bowl and stir.

4. Using a spoon, beat in flour until too thick to stir. Then, use hands to mix in remaining flour.

5. Knead bread dough until smooth and elastic.

6. Cover with towel or plastic wrap and set in a warm place to rise. Let rise for 1 hour, or until dough doubles in size.

7. Using fists, punch dough down and remove from bowl.

8. Shape dough into 5 loaves.

9. Place loaves into well-greased loaf pans and let rise for 1 hour, covered, or until dough doubles in size.

10. Bake at 350°F for 30–40 minutes.

REFRIGERATOR BREAD

Makes 2 loaves

Ingredients:

2 packages *or* 2 tablespoons dry, active yeast
2 cups warm (110–112°) water
½ cup sugar
⅓ cup oil
1 egg, beaten
6½–7 cups flour
1 teaspoon salt

Instructions:

1. In large bowl, dissolve yeast in warm water. Let stand until foamy, approximately 2–5 minutes.

2. Stir in sugar and oil.

3. Add egg, flour, and salt. Knead dough until smooth and elastic.

4. Place dough in a greased bowl. Cover and let rise 1–2 hours, or until double in size.

5. With fists, punch down dough.

6. Place dough in well-greased loaf pans.

7. Cover. Let rise for 1–2 hours, or until nearly doubled in size.

8. Bake at 350°F for 30 minutes.

Variation: After punching down dough, place covered bowl of dough in refrigerator. Take out fresh bread dough as needed to make bread or rolls. When using dough from refrigerator, allow at least 2–3 hours for dough to warm up and rise before baking.

WHOLE WHEAT BREAD

Makes 3 loaves

Ingredients:

2½ tablespoons dry, active yeast
2½ cups warm (110–112°F) water, *divided*
1 tablespoon sugar
4 teaspoons salt
2 cups whole wheat flour
½ cup brown sugar
½ cup water
½ cup oil, *or* lard, melted
½ cup molasses, *or* honey
4–5 cups white flour

Instructions:

1. In large bowl, dissolve yeast in 2 cups water.

2. Add sugar, salt, and whole wheat flour. Mix well.

3. Let stand for 1 hour.

4. Add brown sugar, ½ cup water, oil, and molasses. Stir together.

5. Add white flour until dough is smooth and elastic.

6. Cover with towel or plastic wrap and let rise for 1 hour, or until dough is double in size.

7. With fists, punch down dough.

8. Shape dough into 3 loaves and place in well-greased loaf pans.

9. Cover. Let dough rise for 1 hour, or until dough is double in size.

10. Bake at 350°F for 35 minutes.

Tip: For faster rising time, place the covered bowl in the oven. Keep oven off. The warmth of the pilot light helps dough rise faster.

OATMEAL BREAD

Makes 3 loaves

Ingredients:

2 cups boiling water
1 cup dry quick oats
½ cup whole wheat flour
½ cup brown sugar
1 tablespoon salt
2 tablespoons butter, softened
1 tablespoon dry, active yeast
½ cup very warm (110–115°F) water
5 cups all-purpose flour
Melted butter

Instructions:

1. In large bowl, pour 2 cups boiling water over dry oatmeal.

2. Stir in whole wheat flour, sugar, salt, and butter. Allow to cool.

3. In a separate bowl, dissolve yeast in ½ cup very warm water.

4. Add yeast to oatmeal mixture.

5. Add all-purpose flour and beat until creamy.

6. Knead dough until smooth and elastic.

7. Cover dough with towel or plastic wrap, and let rise for 1 hour.

8. With fists, punch down dough.

9. Shape into 3 loaves and put into well-greased loaf pans.

10. Cover. Allow dough to rise for 1 hour, or until dough has doubled in size.

11. Bake at 350°F for 30 minutes.

12. When done baking, brush tops of loaves with melted butter.

POTATO ROLLS

Makes 12 rolls

Ingredients:

1 cup warm (110–112°F) water
1 tablespoon dry, active yeast
½ cup oil
1 cup mashed potatoes
½ cup sugar
2 eggs
½ teaspoon salt
5–5½ cups Occident,* or all-purpose, flour

*Occident flour is bread flour made from western wheat.

Instructions:

1. In small bowl, mix together water and yeast. Let stand 15 minutes.

2. In a large bowl, stir together oil, mashed potatoes, sugar, eggs, and salt.

3. Add yeast mixture.

4. Stir in flour and knead until smooth. Dough will be sticky.

5. Cover and let rise for 2 hours.

6. Using hands, shape dough into rolls.

7. Place in well-greased cake pan or cupcake pan. Cover. Let rise 1–1½ hours, or until dough has doubled in size.

8. Bake at 350° until rolls are golden brown, about 15–20 minutes.

DINNER ROLLS

Makes 12–18 rolls

Ingredients:

2 tablespoons dry, active yeast
½ cup warm (110–112°F) water
1 cup scalded milk
1 tablespoon salt
½ cup sugar
½ cup (1 stick) butter, melted
2 eggs, beaten
5½ cups flour, *divided*
Melted butter for top

Instructions:

1. Dissolve yeast in warm water and let stand.

2. In medium pan, heat milk until almost boiling.

3. Add salt, sugar, and butter to milk.

4. Cool milk mixture until lukewarm, 80–85°F.

5. Stir in yeast mixture and eggs.

6. Add flour, stirring in as much as you can until well mixed.

7. Knead in remaining flour, or as much as you can, until dough is smooth and elastic.

8. Place dough in well-greased bowl. Cover and let rise 1–2 hours, or until dough is double in size.

9. Form dough into rolls and place on well-greased cookie sheet or jelly-roll pan, approximately 2 inches apart.

10. Cover. Allow dough to rise 1–2 hours, or until dough is double in size.

11. Bake at 350°F for 20–30 minutes, until rolls are light brown.

12. Brush tops of rolls with melted butter before taking off cookie sheet.

CONVERSION CHARTS

METRIC AND IMPERIAL CONVERSIONS

(These conversions are rounded for convenience)

Ingredient	Cups/Tablespoons/ Teaspoons	Ounces	Grams/Milliliters
Butter	1 cup/ 16 tablespoons/ 2 sticks	8 ounces	230 grams
Cheese, shredded	1 cup	4 ounces	110 grams
Chicken, chopped or diced	1 cup	4.4 ounces	125 grams
Cream cheese	1 tablespoon	0.5 ounce	14.5 grams
Cornstarch	1 tablespoon	0.3 ounce	8 grams
Flour, all-purpose	1 cup/1 tablespoon	4.5 ounces/0.3 ounce	125 grams/8 grams
Flour, whole wheat	1 cup	4 ounces	120 grams
Fruit, dried	1 cup	4 ounces	120 grams
Fruits or veggies, chopped	1 cup	5 to 7 ounces	145 to 200 grams
Fruits or veggies, pureed	1 cup	8.5 ounces	245 grams
Honey, maple syrup, or corn syrup	1 tablespoon	0.75 ounce	20 grams
Liquids: broth, cream, milk, water, or juice	1 cup	8 fluid ounces	240 milliliters
Meat	1 pound	16 ounces	453.6 grams
Oats	1 cup	5.5 ounces	150 grams
Rice, white, cooked	1 cup	6.18 ounces	175 grams
Salt	1 teaspoon	0.2 ounce	6 grams
Spices: cinnamon, cloves, ginger, or nutmeg (ground)	1 teaspoon	0.2 ounce	5 milliliters
Sugar, brown, firmly packed	1 cup	7 ounces	200 grams
Sugar, white	1 cup/1 tablespoon	7 ounces/0.5 ounce	200 grams/12.5 grams
Vanilla extract	1 teaspoon	0.2 ounce	4 grams

OVEN TEMPERATURES

Fahrenheit	Celsius	Gas Mark
225°	110°	¼
250°	120°	½
275°	140°	1
300°	150°	2
325°	160°	3
350°	180°	4
375°	190°	5
400°	200°	6
425°	220°	7
450°	230°	8

INDEX

ALSO AVAILABLE

AMISH Canning & Preserving

How to Make Soups, Sauces, Pickles, Relishes, and More

Laura Anne Lapp

60 Simple, Classic Recipes

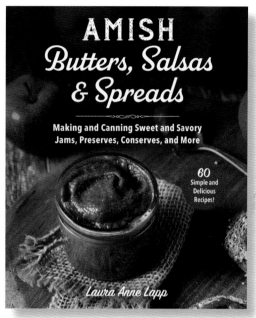

AMISH Butters, Salsas & Spreads

Making and Canning Sweet and Savory Jams, Preserves, Conserves, and More

60 Simple and Delicious Recipes!

Laura Anne Lapp

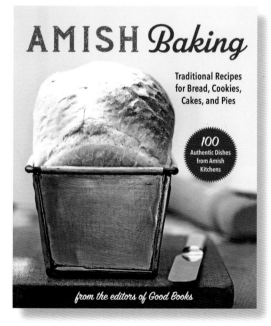

AMISH Baking

Traditional Recipes for Bread, Cookies, Cakes, and Pies

100 Authentic Dishes from Amish Kitchens

from the editors of Good Books

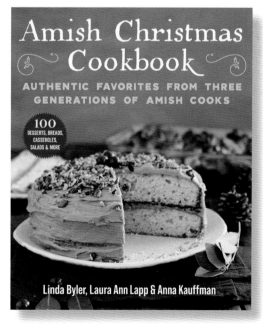

Amish Christmas Cookbook

AUTHENTIC FAVORITES FROM THREE GENERATIONS OF AMISH COOKS

100 DESSERTS, BREADS, CASSEROLES, SALADS & MORE

Linda Byler, Laura Ann Lapp & Anna Kauffman